Classic Essential

❧ ❀ ❧

RICE

KÖNEMANN

～ A Word About Rice ～

Rice dishes can be spicy or tangy, savoury or sweet. Rice soaks up gravies and rich sauces and cools and refreshes the palate when served with spicy food. Baked with milk and sugar, rice transforms itself into one of our best-loved creamy puddings. Rice has no fat, no salt and no sugar but many important nutrients, and is the staple food of over half the world's population. Little wonder, then, that many of the world's finest dishes have been based around it.

In Japan the word for rice, *gohan*, also means the entire meal, while in China people are called to the dinner table by the phrase 'rice is ready'. Indeed, in many Asian countries a meal is considered incomplete without rice. With over half the population of the world eating rice two or three times a day, it is not surprising that there are many arguments over how it should be cooked. Some say you must never lift the lid, while others cook their rice uncovered. One hint that is widely accepted is to always use a big pan. This allows the rice to expand and lie as shallow as possible. Otherwise the lower layers will be crushed, cook faster and become soggy. Several recipes in this book call for cooked rice: a rice cooker will produce perfect rice every time, but if you don't have one, try the following methods.

Fast boiling: Bring a large pan of water to a fast boil. Add the rice and cook, uncovered, for 12 minutes, stirring occasionally (brown rice will take 40 minutes). Drain.

Absorption: Wash 2^1/2 cups (500 g/1 lb) rice in a sieve until the water runs clear. Put in a large pan with 3 cups (750 ml/24 fl oz) water, bring to the boil and boil for 1 minute. Cover tightly, reduce the heat to as low as possible and cook for 10 minutes. Turn off the heat and leave the pan, covered, for 10 minutes. Fluff the rice with a fork.

Long and short grains
There are very many different types of rice. Some are named for their origins but most are distinguished by the size of their grains: long, medium or short. Longer grains contain less starch and remain separate during cooking. Short grains contain more starch and become gluey when cooked so that they stick together. Glutinous rice (also known as 'sweet' or 'sticky') has very high amounts of starch. In some recipes, rice is fried in oil or butter until translucent before adding any liquid. The oil then impregnates the outer layers of the rice and keeps the grains separate. Always use the type specified in the recipe (see pages 4–5).

To Rinse or Not?
You will find in some of the recipes in this book the rice is rinsed before

cooking. This will get rid of any powdered starch clinging to the grains, but is not really necessary to clean the rice: today's packaged varieties should be clean. Some of the starchy short-grain rices are rinsed before cooking to make the grains separate a little rather than sticking together. You will notice, for instance, that the rice is rinsed for *Sushi* but not for *Arancini* where a more sticky consistency is needed. Some long-grain brown rices are soaked before cooking to reduce the cooking time.

How Much Water?

Rice just about trebles in bulk when cooked and this is by absorbing water. Most of us have experienced the unpleasant realisation that our rice has boiled dry and welded itself to the base of the pan. We would love to have a failsafe rule for preventing this, but unfortunately there can be no strict water to rice ratio for cooking long-grain rice: the greater the quantity of rice, the less water is needed proportionately. The Chinese solve this conundrum by putting rice in a pan, resting

their fingertip lightly on it and adding water up to the first finger joint. As a very general rule, long-grain rice will absorb about three times its bulk in water, while short-grain will take far more. Short-grain pudding rice swells and will absorb large amounts of milk to give a creamy consistency. Arborio rice absorbs a great deal of cooking liquid, so taking on its flavour, but without becoming too soft. Because every batch of rice absorbs varying amounts of liquid we cannot give exact stock quantities for risottos.

～ Rice Varieties ～

Now that so many varieties are available to us, it is easy to create the world's favourite rice dishes in our own kitchens.

White Short-grain
Small oval grains of high-starch rice. The large amount of starch is responsible for the grains clinging together during cooking. It is the preferred rice in Japan for Sushi and in Spain for Paella.

Brown Short-grain
A short-grain rice used for risotto, desserts, soups and patties. Delicious nutty flavour with a wet, heavy texture. A healthy alternative to white rice

although purists prefer long-grain. Cook using the absorption method or fry in butter before

adding liquid (for risotto). Brown rice takes much longer to cook than white because it takes considerable time for the water to break through the tough bran layer.

Brown Long-grain
These are separate long grains with husks, best used for salads, rice cakes, pilaf and patties or for serving with stir-fries or curries. A healthy alternative to long-grain white.

White Long-grain
Chosen above other rices by the Chinese. This could stem from Confucius' insistence on eating it. It is grown in the monsoon region of South-East Asia and is often referrred to as water rice. Long-grain white

rice has been processed to remove the outer hull and bran, then polished

until it is white and glossy. A teaspoon or two of lemon juice added to the water will make the rice whiter after cooking.

Arborio
Arborio takes its name from a village in the Piedmont region of northern Italy where it was originally grown. Used for risotto, the grain is first cooked in butter or oil. Once liquid is added (which should always be

simmering and added very gradually) the rice begins to swell and produce a wonderful creamy sauce. Even after cooking, Arborio should always retain a slight 'bite' in the centre.

Basmati

An elegant long-grain rice with a lovely fragrance, grown in India on the foothills of the Himalayas, but now popular throughout the world. Traditionally used in biriani and pilaf,

where saffron is added to give colour and flavour. When used as an accompaniment to Indian dishes, add a bay leaf to the cooking water to lift the flavour of the rice.

Wild Rice

Not a rice but the grain of a water grass, native to the Great Lakes of North America. Grown originally by the Chippewa Indians and harvested by hand, it is now also farmed by machine. It has slender dark brown grains, a delicious nutty flavour and a distinguishable chewy texture. Wild rice requires thorough washing before use. It can be bought in small packets and is considered expensive compared to other rices. It is now available mixed with brown rice and sold as a wild rice blend which is more economical.

Jasmine

Long-grain fragrant white rice used throughout South-East Asia. Usually steamed or cooked using the absorption method and then served as an accompaniment to all Thai meals.

Black Glutinous

A long-grain rice used for Asian desserts and snacks. Ill-named, as it contains no gluten but has a high amount of starch. Normally soaked before boiling. Grown in Indonesia and the Philippines.

White Glutinous

Like black glutinous, this does not contain gluten but a large amount of starch. Soak before steaming.

Usually served as a dessert, but some Asian countries (Laos) use it as an accompaniment to savoury dishes instead of white long-grain.

～ Paella ～

Preparation time:
45 minutes
+ 2 hours soaking
Total cooking time:
50 minutes

Serves 4

---

12 mussels, scrubbed,
  beards removed
1/2 cup (125 ml/4 fl oz)
  white wine
1 small red onion,
  chopped
1/3 cup (80 ml/2 3/4 fl oz)
  olive oil
1 small chicken breast
  fillet, cut into cubes
280 g (9 oz) raw
  prawns, peeled
  and deveined
90 g (3 oz) calamari, cut
  into rings
90 g (3 oz) white
  boneless fish, cut
  into pieces
1/2 small red onion,
  extra, finely chopped

1 rasher bacon, finely
  chopped
4 cloves garlic, crushed
1 small red capsicum,
  finely chopped
1 tomato, peeled, seeded
  and chopped
1/2 cup (80 g/2 2/3 oz)
  fresh or frozen peas
90 g (3 oz) chorizo or
  pepperoni, sliced
pinch cayenne pepper
1 cup (200 g/6 1/2 oz)
  long-grain rice
1/4 teaspoon powdered
  saffron
2 cups (500 ml/16 fl oz)
  hot chicken stock
2 tablespoons finely
  chopped fresh parsley

---

1. ～Soak the cleaned mussels for 2 hours in cold water. Discard any that are open. Heat the wine and onion in a large pan. Add the mussels, cover and shake the pan for 3–5 minutes over high heat. After 3 minutes start removing the opened mussels and set aside; after 5 minutes discard any unopened mussels. Reserve the wine and onion mixture.

2. ～In a large frying pan heat half the oil. Dry the chicken with paper towels, then cook for 5 minutes, or until golden brown. Remove and set aside. Add the prawns, calamari and fish to the pan and cook for 1 minute. Remove and set aside.

3. ～Heat the remaining oil in the pan; add the extra onion, bacon, garlic and capsicum. Cook for 5 minutes, or until the onion is soft.

Add the tomato, peas, chorizo or pepperoni, cayenne pepper and salt and pepper to taste. Add the reserved wine and onion mixture and stir to combine. Add the rice and mix well.

4. ～Blend the saffron with 1/2 cup (125 ml/ 4 fl oz) stock; add to the rice mixture with the remaining stock and mix well. Bring slowly to the boil and then reduce the heat to low and simmer, uncovered, 15 minutes without stirring.

5. ～Place the chicken, prawns, calamari and fish on top of the rice.

Using a wooden spoon, gently push the pieces into the rice, then cover and continue to cook over low heat for 10–15 minutes, or until the rice is tender and the seafood cooked. If the rice is not quite cooked, add a little extra stock and cook for a few minutes more. Serve Paella in bowls, topped with mussels and sprinkled with parsley.
Note ～It's a good idea to buy a few extra mussels to allow for any that do not open. Both black and green lip mussels are suitable.

As the mussels open, remove them from the pan. Discard any that don't open.

Blend the saffron into the stock and then add to the pan. Mix well.

~ Dolmades ~

Preparation time:
**1 hour
+ 1 hour soaking**
Total cooking time:
55 minutes

Makes about 35

250 g (8 oz) vine leaves in brine	**¹/3 cup (20 g/²/3 oz) coarsely chopped fresh dill**
³/4 cup (185 ml/6 fl oz) olive oil	**1 tablespoon finely chopped fresh mint**
2 large onions, finely chopped	**1¹/2 cups (375 ml/ 12 fl oz) water**
³/4 cup (165 g/5¹/2 oz) short-grain rice	**1 tablespoon lemon juice**
6 spring onions, chopped	

1~Rinse the vine leaves in cold water, soak in warm water for 1 hour and then drain. Use five or six of the vine leaves to line the base of a large heavy-based pan.

2~Heat ¹/2 cup (125 ml/4 fl oz) oil in a small heavy-based pan. Add the onion and cook over low heat for 5 minutes. Remove from the heat and leave covered for 5 minutes. Add the rice, spring onions and herbs, mix well and season to taste with salt and pepper.

3~Lay out a vine leaf, vein-side up, on a board or plate. Place 3 teaspoons of filling onto the centre of the leaf. Fold the sides over the mixture, then roll up towards the tip of the leaf. Repeat with the remaining filling and vine leaves.

4~Arrange the Dolmades in the lined pan in two layers and drizzle with the remaining oil. Put a plate on top of the Dolmades to keep them in place and cover with water. Bring to the boil, reduce the heat and simmer, covered, for 45 minutes. Remove the plate, lift out the Dolmades with a slotted spoon and drizzle with lemon juice. Serve warm or cold.

Note~Fresh vine leaves can be used in this recipe if available. Use small leaves, blanched briefly in boiling water.

Use five or six vine leaves to line the base of a large pan.

Place 3 teaspoons of filling into the centre of each leaf.

Roll up the vine leaf, folding in the sides to enclose the filling in a neat parcel.

Arrange the Dolmades in a double layer in the lined pan.

~ Nasi Goreng ~

Preparation time:
40 minutes
Total cooking time:
20 minutes

Serves 4–6

1 ~ Heat the oil in a wok; swirl to coat base. Pour in the combined egg and soy sauce. Slowly move the wok around, spreading the egg in a thin layer. Cook until just set and lightly coloured underneath. Remove with a spatula, roll up tightly and slice into thin strips. Cover and set aside.

2 ~ **To make Nasi Goreng:** Mix together the ginger, turmeric, shrimp paste, chilli sauce and salt. Heat the oil in a large wok; add the onion and garlic and stir-fry over high heat for 1–2 minutes. Add the ginger mixture and continue to cook for 2–3 minutes. Add the capsicum, celery, carrot, peas and pork and cook for 2–3 minutes, stirring continuously. Add the bean sprouts and cabbage and stir-fry for 2 minutes.

3 ~ Add the rice and prawns and stir-fry over

1 teaspoon oil
2 eggs, lightly beaten
1 teaspoon soy sauce

Nasi Goreng
2–3 teaspoons grated ginger
1 teaspoon ground turmeric
1–1½ teaspoons shrimp paste (blachan or trassi)
1–2 tablespoons chilli sauce, to taste
½ teaspoon salt
3 tablespoons oil
1 large onion, finely chopped
2–3 cloves garlic, crushed
½ red capsicum, chopped
½ celery stick, chopped
1 small carrot, chopped

½ cup (80 g/2⅔ oz) peas
125 g (4 oz) barbecue pork, diced
125 g (4 oz) bean sprouts
2 cups (90 g/3 oz) finely shredded Chinese cabbage
6 cups (1 kg/2 lb) cooked, cold Jasmine rice
125 g (4 oz) cooked peeled prawns, halved
¼ cup (60 g/2 fl oz) coconut cream
1–2 tablespoons kecap manis
½ teaspoon tamarind purée, optional
coriander leaves, to garnish

high heat 3–4 minutes, or until well combined and heated through. Stir constantly to prevent sticking and burning. Combine the coconut cream, kecap manis and tamarind and stir through the rice. Serve immediately, garnished with the egg strips and coriander.

Note ~ Shrimp paste, kecap manis (Indonesian sweet soy sauce), tamarind purée and barbecue pork are all available from Asian food stores.

Variation ~ Instead of, or in addition to, egg strips, another popular garnish for this dish is onion flakes. Heat 2 teaspoons oil in a small pan. Add 20 g (⅔ oz) dried onion flakes all at once and fry for 15–20 seconds, then remove. Drain on paper towels. Or, instead of flakes, thinly slice an onion into rings and fry until well browned.

Slowly move the wok around so the egg spreads out in a thin layer.

Add the mixture of ginger, turmeric, shrimp paste, chilli sauce and salt.

～ Sushi ～

Preparation time:
40 minutes + standing
Total cooking time:
10 minutes

Makes about 30

1.～To make Vinegar Rice: Rinse the rice under running water, until the water runs clear. Put the rice and 2 cups (500 ml/16 fl oz) water in a pan and soak for 10 minutes. Cover and bring to the boil, then reduce the heat to low and simmer gently for 8–10 minutes. Remove from the heat and leave for 15 minutes with the lid on.
2.～Spread the rice in a shallow dish and cool to room temperature. Put the vinegar, sugar and salt in a small pan. Heat gently and sprinkle over the rice. Use at once.

Vinegar Rice
2 cups (440 g/14 oz) short-grain rice
2 tablespoons rice vinegar
2 tablespoons caster sugar
1/2 teaspoon salt
2 teaspoons rice vinegar, extra

5 sheets nori seaweed
wasabi paste, to taste
125 g (4 oz) sashimi tuna or smoked salmon
Japanese pickled ginger and vegetables, finely sliced cucumber and spring onion, to taste

---

3.～Combine the extra rice vinegar with 3 tablespoons water and use to keep your hands moist. Place a sheet of seaweed, shiny-side-down, on a sheet of non-stick baking paper or a bamboo mat if you have one. Spread one-fifth of the rice over a third of the nori sheet, leaving a 2 cm (3/4 inch) border. Spread a very thin layer of wasabi paste in a narrow line down the centre of the rice. Cut the fish into thin strips and place on top of the wasabi. Top with ginger, vegetables, cucumber or spring onion, to taste.
4.～Using the paper or bamboo mat as a guide, roll up the seaweed to enclose the filling. Press to seal the edges. Using a very sharp knife, cut the roll into 2.5 cm (1 inch) rounds. Repeat with the remaining filling and sheets of nori.
Storage time.～Sushi rolls can be made up to 6 hours in advance, stored, covered, in the refrigerator and cut just before serving.

Put the rice in a colander and rinse until the water runs clear.

Spread a fifth of the rice over a third of a sheet of nori.

Spread a very thin layer of wasabi paste along the centre of the rice.

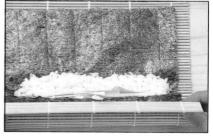

Use the bamboo mat to help you roll up the seaweed to enclose the rice filling.

~ Arancini ~
(Rice Croquettes)

Preparation time:
45 minutes + chilling
Total cooking time:
45 minutes

Makes 10

2 cups (440 g/14 oz)
  short-grain rice
1 egg, lightly beaten
1 egg yolk
1/2 cup (50 g/12/3 oz)
  grated Parmesan

Meat Sauce
1 dried porcini
  mushroom
1 tablespoon olive oil
1 small onion, chopped
125 g (4 oz) minced beef
  or veal

2 slices prosciutto,
  finely chopped
2 tablespoons tomato
  paste
100 ml (31/2 fl oz) white
  wine
1/2 teaspoon dried
  thyme leaves
3 tablespoons finely
  chopped parsley

plain flour
2 eggs, lightly beaten
dry breadcrumbs

1. ⁓Cook the rice in boiling salted water for 20 minutes, or until just soft. Drain, without rinsing, and cool. Put in a large bowl and stir in the egg, egg yolk and Parmesan. Stir until the rice sticks together. Cover and set aside.

2. ⁓**To make Meat Sauce:** Soak the mushroom in hot water for 10 minutes to soften, squeeze dry and chop finely. Heat the oil in a frying pan. Add the mushroom and onion; cook for 2–3 minutes until soft. Add the meat and cook, stirring, for

2–3 minutes until browned. Add the prosciutto, tomato paste, wine, thyme and pepper to taste. Cook, stirring, for 5 minutes, or until all the liquid is absorbed. Stir in the parsley. Set aside to cool.

3. ⁓With wet hands, form the rice mixture into 10 balls. Wet your hands again, pull the balls apart and place

3 heaped teaspoons of Meat Sauce in the centre of each. Remould to enclose the filling; roll in flour, beaten egg and then breadcrumbs. Chill for 1 hour.

4. ⁓Deep-fry the croquettes in oil, two at a time, for 3–4 minutes, or until golden brown. Drain on paper towels and keep warm while frying the remainder.

Pull the rice balls apart and place Meat Sauce in the centre of each.

Roll the rice balls in flour, beaten egg and then breadcrumbs.

～ Mushroom Risotto ～

Preparation time:
**20 minutes +
30 minutes soaking**
Total cooking time:
35–40 minutes

Serves 4–6

20 g (2/3 oz) dried porcini mushrooms	**100 g (3 1/3 oz) baby mushrooms, finely chopped**
1 litre chicken stock	**250 g (8 oz) arborio rice**
60 g (2 oz) butter	**1/2 cup (50 g/1 2/3 oz) grated Parmesan**
2 tablespoons olive oil	**2 tablespoons finely chopped parsley**
1 small onion, finely chopped	
1 clove garlic, crushed	

1. ～Put the porcini mushrooms in a small heatproof bowl and cover with boiling water. Leave for 30 minutes, then drain, reserving 1/2 cup (125 ml/4 fl oz) of the liquid. Squeeze the mushrooms dry with your hands and then chop finely.
2. ～Put the stock and reserved mushroom liquid in a pan and heat to simmering point. In another heavy-based pan, heat the butter and oil and then add the onion, garlic, fresh mushrooms and porcini mushrooms. Cook, stirring, for 3–4 minutes, or until the onion is soft. Add the rice and cook, stirring, for 1–2 minutes, until the rice is well coated but not browned.
3. ～Maintain the stock at simmering point. Add 1/2 cup (125 ml/4 fl oz) of hot stock to the rice mixture. Stir constantly over low heat, with a wooden spoon, until all the liquid has been absorbed, then add more stock. Repeat the process until the rice is creamy and all the stock has been added (only add the last 1/2 cup of stock if needed to finish cooking the rice). This will take 20–25 minutes. Gently stir through the Parmesan and parsley and then serve at once, topped with extra Parmesan, if liked.
Note. ～Arborio rice is a short-grained rice from the Po Valley of Italy. It is very absorbent, so perfect for risotto, and available from most supermarkets. Porcini mushrooms are Italian dried field mushrooms, available from pasta suppliers and some Italian delicatessens.

Squeeze the mushrooms dry with your hands and then chop finely.

Heat the butter and oil, then add the onion, garlic, fresh and porcini mushrooms.

Add the rice to the pan and stir until well-coated but not browned.

The secret of good risotto is to add the stock gradually, stirring until absorbed.

～ Risotto Parmesan ～

Preparation time:
20 minutes
Total cooking time:
40 minutes

Serves 4–6

1 litre chicken stock	1 teaspoon grated
60 g (2 oz) butter	lemon rind
2 tablespoons olive oil	2 teaspoons lemon juice
1 small red onion, finely	1/2 cup (50 g/1 2/3 oz)
chopped	grated Parmesan
1 clove garlic, crushed	2 tablespoons finely
pinch of saffron powder	chopped parsley
250 g (8 oz) arborio rice	Parmesan shavings

1 ～ Put the stock in a pan and maintain at simmering point. In another heavy-based pan, heat the butter and oil. Add the red onion, garlic and saffron and cook, stirring, for 2–3 minutes. Add the rice and cook, stirring, for 1–2 minutes, until the rice is well coated.
2 ～ Add the lemon rind, juice and 1/2 cup (125 ml/4 fl oz) hot stock. Stir over low heat until absorbed, then add more stock. Repeat until all the stock has been added and the rice is tender (25–30 minutes).
3 ～ Stir through the Parmesan and parsley and serve immediately with Parmesan shavings.

～ Risotto Primavera ～

Preparation time:
25 minutes
Total cooking time:
40 minutes

Serves 4–6

1 cup (155 g/5 oz)	1 carrot, finely diced
frozen peas	1 red onion, chopped
155 g (5 oz) thin	1/2 celery stick, diced
asparagus, cut into	1 zucchini, finely diced
short lengths	250 g (8 oz) arborio rice
1 litre chicken stock	1/2 cup (50 g/1 2/3 oz)
60 g (2 oz) butter	grated Parmesan
2 tablespoons olive oil	

1 ～ Cook the peas and asparagus in boiling water for 1–2 minutes, then drain and set aside.
2 ～ Put the stock in a pan and maintain at simmering point. Heat the butter and oil in a heavy-based pan. Add the carrot, onion, celery and zucchini and stir for 2–3 minutes. Remove half the vegetables; set aside. Add the rice to the pan; stir for 1–2 minutes until well coated.
3 ～ Add 1/2 cup (125 ml/4 fl oz) hot stock; stir over low heat until absorbed, then add more stock. Repeat until all the stock has been added and the rice is tender and creamy (25–30 minutes).
4 ～ Stir through the Parmesan, peas, asparagus and reserved vegetables. Serve at once, with extra Parmesan, if liked.

Risotto Parmesan (top) and Risotto Primavera

~ Three Rice Salad ~

Preparation time:
50 minutes +
2 hours marinating
Total cooking time:
50 minutes

Serves 6–8

3/4 cup (150 g/4³/4 oz)
long-grain rice
3/4 cup (165 g/5¹/2 oz)
brown rice
100 g (3¹/3 oz) wild rice
1 red capsicum
1 green capsicum
4 tablespoons olive oil
1 clove garlic, crushed
2 cups (310 g/9³/4 oz)
frozen baby peas

2–3 teaspoons lemon
juice, to taste
pinch of dried mustard
4 tomatoes, peeled,
seeded and chopped
4 spring onions, finely
chopped
1/3 cup (20 g/²/3 oz)
finely chopped parsley
1/3 cup (60 g/2 oz) small
black olives

1 Cook the rices separately, according to the packet instructions. Rinse, drain, cool and set aside.

2 Halve, seed, then quarter the capsicums. Place, skin-side-up, under a hot grill and cook for 8–10 minutes, or until the skin blisters and blackens. Place in a plastic or paper bag for 5 minutes (this will make removing the skin easier). Peel away the skin and discard, then slice the capsicum into thin strips. Combine the oil and garlic in a bowl; add the capsicum strips and leave to marinade for at least 2 hours.

3 Place the peas in a large pan of boiling salted water and cook for 2 minutes, then cool under cold water and drain. Place the capsicum in a strainer and leave to drain over a bowl to collect the oil. Whisk the oil, lemon juice and mustard together. Add salt and pepper, to taste.

4 Mix together the rice, capsicum, peas, tomatoes and spring onions. Stir through the dressing and parsley. Spoon onto a platter and scatter with olives.

Note Wild rice is an aquatic grass rather than a rice. The American Indians were living on it in the Great Lakes region and, because it grows out of the water like rice in a paddy field, early explorers mistook it for such. Even today, most wild rice is still harvested by American Indians using old-fashioned methods.

Grill the capsicum until the skin is blackened and then peel away.

Put the capsicum in a strainer and drain over a bowl to collect the oil.

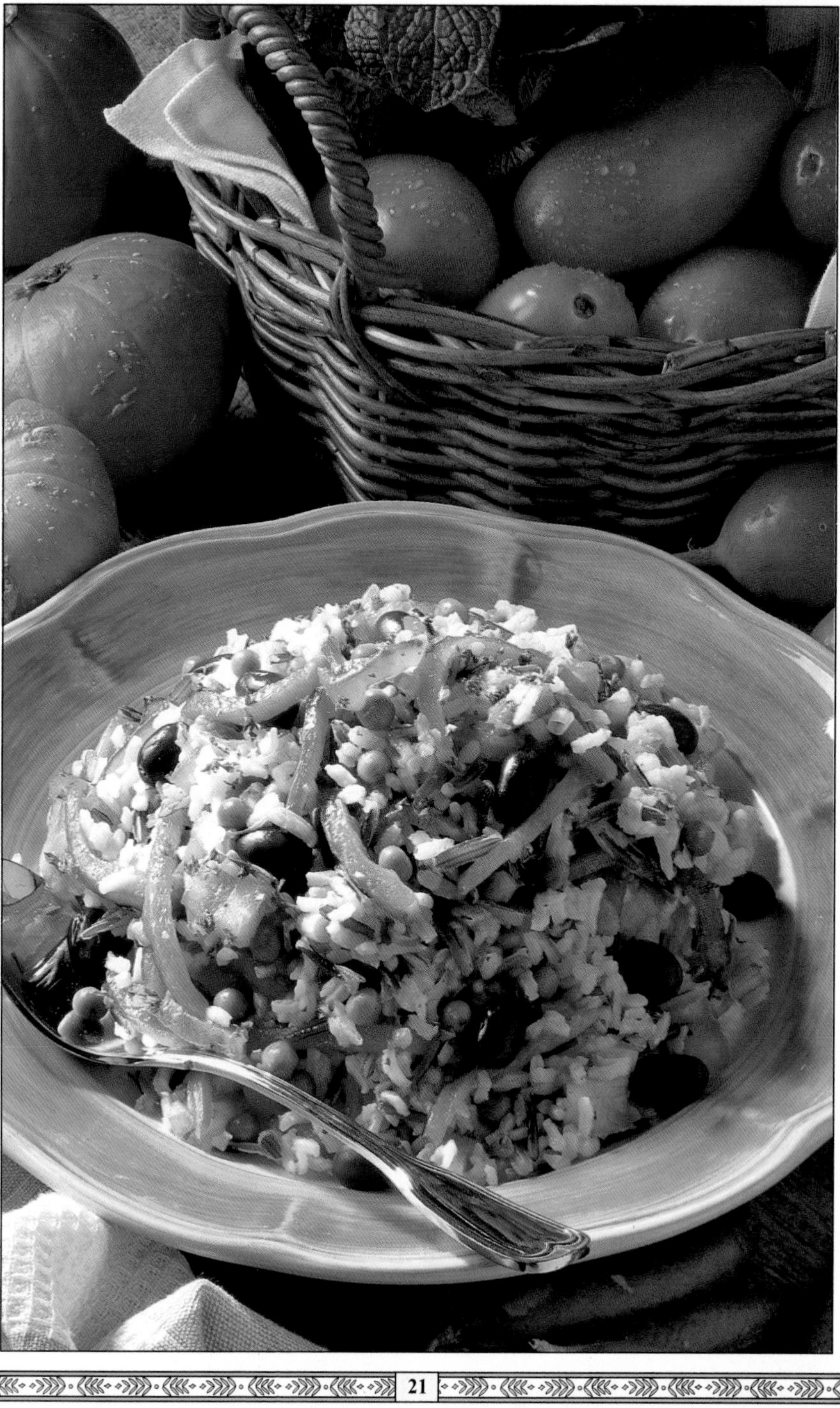

～ Kitchri ～
(Rice and Lentils)

Preparation time:
25 minutes
Total cooking time:
1 hour

Serves 4–6

1 cup (200 g/6¹/2 oz) long-grain basmati rice	1 teaspoon salt
1 cup (250 g/8 oz) red lentils	2 teaspoons garam masala
3 tablespoons ghee	3¹/2 cups (875 ml/ 28 fl oz) hot water
1 large onion, sliced	1 medium onion, sliced

1 ～ Wash the rice two or three times and then drain. Wash the lentils and drain. In a large heavy-based pan, heat 2 tablespoons ghee and add the onion. Cook, stirring frequently, over low heat for 10 minutes, or until golden.

2 ～ Add the rice and lentils and stir over the heat for 2–3 minutes. Add the salt and garam masala and stir for 1 minute, then slowly add the hot water. Bring to the boil, stirring, then reduce the heat to very low and cover with a tight-fitting lid. Cook for 20–25 minutes, checking after about 20 minutes.

3 ～ Heat the remaining ghee in a small frying pan, add the medium onion and cook over moderate heat for 10 minutes, or until golden. Drain on paper towels. Serve the rice and lentils immediately with extra fried onion as a garnish.

Note ～ Serve in place of plain rice with any Indian style dish, such as meat and vegetable curries. To make your own garam masala, put 4 tablespoons coriander seeds, 3 tablespoons cardamom pods, 2 tablespoons cumin seeds, 1 tablespoon whole black peppercorns, 1 teaspoon whole cloves and 3 cinnamon sticks in a small pan. Dry-fry over moderate heat until the spices just start to smell fragrant, then transfer to a plate. Peel the cardamom pods, retaining the seeds only. Put the fried spices in a food processor or blender with a grated whole fresh nutmeg and process into a powder. Store in an airtight jar.

Add the rice and lentils to the ghee and onion in the pan.

Slowly add the hot water and then bring to the boil, stirring continuously.

Cook the sliced onion in ghee for 10 minutes, or until golden.

To make your own garam masala, dry-fry the spices over medium heat.

~ Stuffed Cabbage Rolls ~

Preparation time:
50 minutes
Total cooking time:
2 hours

Serves 4

		Tomato Sauce

1 large Savoy cabbage
2 tablespoons olive oil
1 onion, finely chopped
2 cloves garlic, crushed
250 g (8 oz) pork and
   veal mince
150 g (4^3/4 oz) ham,
   chopped
^{1}/2 cup (110 g/3^2/3 oz)
   short-grain rice
^{1}/2 cup (30 g/1 oz)
   chopped parsley
2 tablespoons chopped
   capers
1 tablespoon malt
   vinegar
1 tablespoon soft brown
   sugar
1 teaspoon allspice

Tomato Sauce
1 tablespoon olive oil
1 small onion, finely
   chopped
425 g (13^1/2 oz) can
   crushed tomatoes
3 tablespoons tomato
   paste
^{1}/2 cup (125 ml/4 fl oz)
   white wine
1 teaspoon dried thyme
   leaves
1 teaspoon caster
   sugar
30 g (1 oz) butter,
   cubed

1 ~ Grease an ovenproof dish, about 30 x 20 x 8 cm (12 x 8 x 3 inches) with melted butter. Preheat the oven to warm 160°C (315°F/Gas 2–3). Cut a circle about 5 cm (2 inches) deep around core end of the cabbage. Carefully remove 8 outer cabbage leaves (discard the inside of the cabbage, or use for coleslaw). Place the whole leaves, in batches, in a large pan of boiling salted water for 2 minutes, or until just wilted. Drain.

2 ~ Heat the oil in a medium pan and cook the onion and garlic for 2–3 minutes, or until softened. Add the mince and mash with a fork. Cook for a further 2–3 minutes. Add the ham and rice and cook, stirring, for a further 2 minutes. Remove from the heat and place in a bowl. Combine the rice mixture with the parsley, capers, vinegar, brown sugar and allspice.

3 ~ Divide the filling into 8 even portions. Cut away the hard centre rib of each cabbage leaf. Overlap the cut pieces of leaf to form larger pieces. Place a portion of filling on each leaf piece, fold in the end and sides, then roll up into a neat parcel, about 12 cm (5 inches) long, enclosing the filling. Place, seam-side-down, in the dish. Put the rolls close together in the dish. If any gaps remain between the rolls use leftover leaves to fill them in.

4 ~ **To make Tomato Sauce:** Heat the oil in a pan, add the onion and cook for 2–3 minutes, without browning. Add the crushed tomatoes, tomato paste, wine, thyme and sugar. Stir to combine and cook for 10 minutes, then pour over the rolls. Dot with butter, then cover the dish tightly with a lid or foil. Bake for 1^1/2 hours, or until the rolls are cooked and tender.

Note ~ Try minced beef or lamb instead of pork and veal. Purée the sauce if you prefer it smooth. Refrigerate for up to 2 days.

Put the cabbage leaves in a large pan of boiling salted water until just wilted.

Roll up the cabbage leaves into a neat parcel to enclose the filling.

～ Jambalaya ～

Preparation time:
30 minutes
Total cooking time:
1 hour

Serves 4–6

1.～Heat the oil in a large heavy-based pan and add the onion, garlic and bacon. Cook, stirring continuously, for 5 minutes, or until the onion is tender. Stir in the rice and cook, stirring, for 2 more minutes, or until well coated.

2.～Add the capsicum, ham, tomatoes, tomato purée, Worcestershire sauce, Tabasco and thyme. Stir for 1 minute until well combined and then bring to the boil. Reduce the heat to very low, cover with a tight-fitting lid and cook for 40 minutes.

2 tablespoons olive oil
1 large red onion, finely chopped
1–2 cloves garlic, crushed
2 rashers bacon, finely chopped
1½ cups (300 g/9²/₃ oz) long-grain rice
1 red or green capsicum, diced
150 g (4³/₄ oz) ham, chopped
425 g (13½ oz) can chopped tomatoes
425 g (13½ oz) can tomato purée
1 teaspoon Worcestershire sauce
dash of Tabasco
½ teaspoon dried thyme
½ cup (30 g/1 oz) chopped parsley
250 g (8 oz) small cooked and peeled prawns
4 spring onions, finely chopped, to garnish

3.～Test the rice—if it is not quite cooked, cover and cook for a further 5–10 minutes, or until tender. Stir in the parsley and cooked prawns. Add salt and freshly ground black pepper to taste. Serve immediately, piled onto a large warm serving plate and garnished with the finely chopped spring onions.

Note.～You will need to buy about 500 g (1 lb) of unpeeled cooked prawns to yield 250 g (8 oz) when peeled. Small school prawns are best for this recipe.

Cook the onion, garlic and bacon and then stir in the rice until well coated.

Add the capsicum, ham, tomatoes, purée, Worcestershire sauce, Tabasco and thyme.

～ Avgolemono ～
(Greek Egg and Lemon Soup)

Preparation time:
20 minutes
Total cooking time:
15 minutes

Serves 4–6

6 cups (1.5 litres) chicken stock	**2 eggs, separated**
3/4 cup (150 g/4 3/4 oz) white, long-grain rice	**1/2 cup (125 ml/4 fl oz) lemon juice**

1～Bring the stock to the boil in a large pan. Add the rice and simmer for 12–15 minutes, or until tender.
2～Beat the egg whites in a small dry mixing bowl until soft peaks form. Add the yolks and beat until combined. Gradually pour the lemon juice, then 2 cups (500 ml/16 fl oz) of the hot stock and rice, into the egg mixture, beating constantly. Pour this quickly into the pan of cooked rice and stock; stir through and serve.

Note～Egg and Lemon Soup, one of the most renowned dishes of Greek cuisine, can also be made with fish stock. Assemble the ingredients and utensils beforehand, work quickly and serve immediately as this soup does not reheat well.

～ Kedgeree ～

Preparation time:
20 minutes
Total cooking time:
12 minutes

Serves 4

500 g (1 lb) smoked haddock or cod	**3 cups (555 g/ 1 lb 2 oz) cooked basmati rice, kept hot**
1 piece lemon rind	
1 bay leaf	**1/3 cup (20 g/2/3 oz) finely chopped fresh parsley**
60 g (2 oz) butter	
1 large onion, finely chopped	**2 egg yolks**
1 teaspoon curry powder	**1/4 cup (60 ml/2 fl oz) cream**
3 hard-boiled eggs, chopped	**1 lemon, quartered, to serve**

1～Put the fish in a large pan with the lemon rind and bay leaf. Cover with water. Bring slowly to the boil and then reduce the heat and simmer for 6–8 minutes until cooked. Drain and then remove the skin and bone and flake the fish; set aside.

2～Heat the butter in large frying pan. Add the onion and curry powder. Stir for 5 minutes, or until the onion is soft, but not browned.

3～Add the eggs, cooked rice, flaked fish, parsley and combined egg yolks and cream. Mix until just combined. Serve very hot with lemon quarters.

Avgolemono (top) and Kedgeree

～ Suppli ～

Preparation time:
40 minutes + chilling
Total cooking time:
1 hour

Makes about 20

50 g (1²/₃ oz) butter
1 small onion, finely
  chopped
1²/₃ cups (360 g/
  11¹/₂ oz) arborio rice
¹/₂ cup (125 ml/4 fl oz)
  white wine
pinch of powdered
  saffron
3 cups (750 ml/24 fl oz)
  chicken stock
¹/₂ cup (50 g/1²/₃ oz)
  grated Parmesan
2 eggs, lightly beaten
65 g (2¹/₄ oz)
  mozzarella cheese
dry breadcrumbs
oil, for deep-frying

1 ～Heat the butter in large heavy-based pan. Add the onion and cook for 2–3 minutes until softened but not brown. Add the rice and stir for 2–3 minutes further, until well coated with butter and onion.

2 ～Add the combined wine and saffron and stir until all the wine is absorbed. Put the stock in a pan and maintain at simmering point. Add ¹/₂ cup (125 ml/4 fl oz) stock to the rice and stir continuously until absorbed, then add more stock. Continue until ¹/₂ cup of stock remains (about 15 minutes). Add the remaining stock and stir, then cover with a tight-fitting lid, reduce the heat to very low and cook for 10–15 minutes until the rice is tender. Leave to cool.

3 ～Gently stir through the Parmesan, eggs and salt and pepper to taste. Cut the mozzarella cheese into 20 small cubes. With wet hands, form the rice mixture into egg-sized balls. Push a cube of mozzarella into the centre of each ball and mould the rice around it.

4 ～Coat each ball with breadcrumbs. Chill for at least 1 hour to firm up. Heat the oil in a deep heavy-based pan. Fry 3–4 balls at a time for 4–5 minutes, or until golden brown. Drain on paper towels. Serve hot.

Storage time ～Keep covered and refrigerated for up to 3 days. Reheat in a warm oven for 15 minutes.

Note ～The full name is *Suppli al Telefono*: serve hot so that the cheese filling pulls out into long thin strands like telephone wires when bitten into.

Cook the onion in butter until soft and then add the rice. Stir until well coated.

Mix together the wine and saffron and add to the pan.

Push a cube of mozarella into the centre of each rice ball.

Coat each rice ball with dry breadcrumbs before deep-frying.

～ Lemper ～

(Coconut Rice wrapped in Banana Leaves)

Preparation time:
40 minutes
Total cooking time:
1 hour 30 minutes

Makes about 12

2–3 young banana
  leaves (see note)

Coconut Rice
2 cups (400 g/12²/₃ oz)
  glutinous rice
³/₄ cup (185 ml /6 fl oz)
  coconut milk

Chicken Filling
2 tablespoons oil
2–3 cloves garlic,
  crushed

6 curry leaves
1 teaspoon dried
  shrimp paste
2 teaspoons ground
  coriander
2 teaspoons ground
  cumin
¹/₂ teaspoon turmeric
250 g (8 oz) chicken
  mince
3 tablespoons coconut
  milk, extra
1 teaspoon lemon juice

1～First, prepare the banana leaves. With a sharp knife cut away the central ribs. As they are cut, the leaves will split into large pieces—cut into pieces about 15 cm (6 inches) square. Wash, then pour boiling water over to soften them. Spread out on a tea towel and cover.

2～**To make Coconut Rice:** Wash the rice; drain well. Put in a large heavy-based saucepan with 1³/4 cups (440 ml/14 fl oz) water. Bring slowly to the boil, reduce the heat to very low, cover tightly and cook for 15 minutes.

3～Put the coconut milk and ¹/2 cup (125 ml/4 fl oz) water in a small saucepan and heat through without boiling. Stir through the rice with a fork. Turn out into a bowl, leaving the soft rice on the base of the pan. Set aside and leave to cool.

4～**To make Chicken Filling:** Heat the oil in a large heavy-based frying pan; add the garlic and curry leaves and stir for 1 minute. Add the shrimp paste, coriander, cumin and turmeric and cook for a further minute. Add the chicken mince; cook and mash with a fork for 3–4 minutes, or until the chicken changes colour. Stir in the extra coconut milk and continue to cook over low heat for 5 minutes, or until absorbed. Remove the curry leaves. Add the lemon juice and salt and pepper, to taste. Cool.

5～Place 2 heaped tablespoons of rice into the centre of each leaf piece and flatten to a 5 cm (2 inch) square.

Top with 2 heaped teaspoons of Chicken Filling. Roll up the leaf into a parcel and place, seam-side-down, in a steamer lined with leftover banana leaf scraps. Steam, in batches, for 15 minutes. Serve at room temperature.

Note～If banana leaves are unavailable use squares of foil. Glutinous rice, curry leaves and shrimp paste are all available from Asian stores. Keep Lemper, covered and refrigerated, for up to 2 days.

Heat the coconut milk and water in a small pan and then stir into the rice.

Place 2 heaped teaspoons of filling on top of the rice.

～ Risi e Bisi ～

Preparation time:
20 minutes
Total cooking time:
35 minutes

Serves 4–6

90 g (3 oz) butter
1 onion, finely chopped
1–2 cloves garlic,
  crushed
1 small celery stick,
  finely chopped
2 slices prosciutto,
  chopped
500 g (1 lb) frozen peas
1/2 cup (125 ml/4 fl oz)
  white wine

4 cups (1 litre) beef
  stock
2 cups (440 g/14 oz)
  arborio rice
1/3 cup (35 g/1 1/4 oz)
  grated Parmesan
2 teaspoons chopped
  fresh mint
1/2 cup (30 g/1 oz)
  chopped parsley

1～In a large heavy-based pan, heat 30 g (1 oz) of the butter then add the onion, garlic, celery and prosciutto. Cook over medium heat, stirring occasionally, for 5 minutes, or until the onion is softened.
2～Add the peas and wine and cook for a further 5 minutes over low heat until the wine has been absorbed.
3～In a separate large pan, heat the beef stock and maintain at a low simmer. Add the rice to the onion and pea mixture and stir for 1–2 minutes until the rice is well coated. Add

1/2 cup (125 ml/4 fl oz) of the hot stock. Stir constantly over medium heat until all the stock is absorbed. Add another 1/2 cup of stock and stir until absorbed; repeat until all the stock is added and the rice is creamy but still has a slight bite. This will take about 20 minutes.
4～Remove the pan from the heat; stir in the remaining butter, Parmesan, mint, parsley and freshly ground black pepper to taste.

Note～If the rice is not quite cooked, cover with a tight-fitting lid for 1–2 minutes—the steam will finish off the cooking. The name of the dish translates from Italian as, quite simply, Rice and Peas. Use chicken or vegetable stock instead of the beef stock, if preferred.

Heat the butter in a large pan, then add the onion, garlic, celery and prosciutto.

Add the peas and wine and cook for a further 5 minutes.

Put the stock in a pan and maintain at a low simmer.

Add the stock to the pan, half a cup at a time, and stir continuously.

~ Saffron Rice ~

Preparation time:
20 minutes
Total cooking time:
30 minutes

Serves 4–6

---

1 tablespoon ghee
1 onion, finely chopped
6 whole cloves
6 cardamom pods,
　lightly bruised
6 whole peppercorns
1¼ cups (250 g/8 oz)
　long-grain basmati
　rice
1 cinnamon stick
2 cups (500 ml/16 fl oz)
　hot chicken stock
1 teaspoon grated
　lemon rind
2 tablespoons lemon
　juice
pinch of saffron
　strands

---

1 ~ Heat the ghee in a large heavy-based pan; add the onion and fry for 3 minutes, or until softened but not browned. Add the cloves, cardamom pods, peppercorns, rice and cinnamon stick. Stir for a further 2–3 minutes, over low heat.

2 ~ Add the hot stock, lemon rind and juice. Bring to the boil, reduce the heat to very low, cover with a tight-fitting lid and cook for 10 minutes. Meanwhile, place the saffron strands in a small bowl and add 2 tablespoons boiling water. Set aside for 5 minutes, then squeeze the strands with your fingers to extract all the colour and make the water golden.

3 ~ Pick the saffron strands from the water and sprinkle evenly over the rice. Sprinkle the water evenly over the rice but do not stir. Replace the lid and cook for a further 8 minutes. Uncover to allow the steam to escape for 5 minutes, then gently stir the rice with a fork. Serve at once. Remove the spices from the surface, if preferred.

Note ~ Serve with any Indian style dish such as curry. The colour is very attractive so makes a beautiful special occasion dish. May be garnished with toasted almonds, sultanas and peas, if liked. Saffron strands are expensive but only a pinch is required and the result is far superior to using the powdered variety.

Fry the onion until soft, then add the rice and spices.

Add the hot stock, lemon rind and juice and bring to the boil.

Add 2 tablespoons of boiling water to the saffron strands.

Sprinkle the saffron strands and liquid over the rice but do not stir.

～ Piroshki ～

Preparation time:
50 minutes + chilling
Total cooking time:
25 minutes

Makes about 20

2¹/₂ cups (310 g/9³/₄ oz) plain flour	**1 small onion, finely chopped**
¹/₂ teaspoon salt	**¹/₂ cup (90 g/3 oz) cooked short-grain rice**
180 g (5³/₄ oz) cold butter, cubed	
1 egg yolk	**1 hard-boiled egg, finely chopped**
¹/₄ cup (60 ml/2 fl oz) sour cream	**2 tablespoons finely chopped parsley**
Filling	**2 tablespoons finely chopped dill**
150 g (4³/₄ oz) mushrooms	**1 egg, lightly beaten, to glaze**
50 g (1²/₃ oz) butter	

1～Lightly grease a baking tray with melted butter or oil. Process the flour, salt and butter for 20 seconds or until fine and crumbly. Add the yolk and sour cream and process for 15 seconds, or until the mixture comes together (you may need to add up to 1 tablespoon water). Turn out onto a lightly floured surface and gather together to form a smooth dough. Wrap in plastic wrap and chill for 30 minutes.

2～**To make Filling:** Process the mushrooms until finely chopped. In a heavy-based frying pan, heat the butter. Add the onion and cook for 3 minutes, or until softened. Add the mushrooms and cook, stirring, for a further 3 minutes. Stir in the rice. Transfer to a bowl and cool. Stir through the chopped egg and herbs and season well.

3.～Roll out the pastry thinly, half at a time, on a floured surface. Cut 20 rounds, with an 8 cm (3 inch) plain cutter.

Place a tablespoon of filling in the centre of each round. Brush the pastry edges with egg glaze, fold in half and pinch the edges to seal. Prick the tops with a fork. Place on the tray and chill for 30 minutes. Preheat the oven to moderately hot 190°C (375°F/Gas 5). Brush the pastries with egg and bake for 15 minutes, or until golden. Serve hot as a starter or with soup.

Process the flour, salt and butter until fine crumbs form.

Cook the onion in butter until softened and then add the finely chopped mushrooms.

Roll out half the pastry at a time and cut rounds with a plain cutter.

Place a tablespoon of filling in the centre of each pastry round.

～ Fried Rice ～

Preparation time:
**40 minutes +
marinating**
Total cooking time:
15–20 minutes

Serves 4–6

150 g (4¾ oz) fillet beef
**4 dried Chinese
mushrooms**
3 tablespoons soy sauce
**1 teaspoon soft brown
sugar**
1 teaspoon cornflour
1 tablespoon sesame oil
3 tablespoons peanut oil
**2 teaspoons grated
ginger**
**2–3 cloves garlic,
crushed**
**125 g (4 oz) barbecued
pork or bacon, diced**
**8 spring onions, sliced
on the diagonal**

**125 g (4 oz) green
beans, sliced on
the diagonal**
**1 celery stick, sliced on
the diagonal**
**1 small red or green
capsicum, cut into
thin strips**
**6 cups (1 kg/2 lb)
cooked long-grain rice**
**280 g (9 oz) can baby
corn, drained and cut
into short lengths**
**1 cup (155 g/5 oz)
frozen peas, defrosted**
**125 g (4 oz) small
cooked, peeled prawns**

1 ～ Place the beef in the freezer for 20 minutes to make it easier to slice. Soak the mushrooms in ½ cup (125 ml/4 fl oz) boiling water for 20 minutes; drain and reserve the liquid. Squeeze the mushrooms dry then chop, removing the hard stalk. Set aside.

2 ～ Slice the beef thinly across the grain, then cut into thin strips. In a small bowl, combine the reserved mushroom liquid, soy sauce, brown sugar and cornflour. Add the beef; marinate for 20 minutes. Drain the meat on paper towels, saving the liquid.

3 ～ Heat the sesame oil and 2 tablespoons peanut oil in a wok; add the ginger and garlic. Stir-fry for 2–3 minutes without browning. Increase the heat, add the beef, mushrooms, barbecue pork or bacon and stir-fry over high heat for 2–3 minutes.

4 ～ Transfer the meat mixture to a side plate. Add the remaining oil to the wok and reheat; add the spring onions, beans, celery and capsicum. Stir-fry the vegetables over high heat for 3–4 minutes. Combine the meat and vegetable mixture and stir-fry for a further 1–2 minutes.

5 ～ Add the cooked rice and stir for 2–3 minutes to combine all the ingredients. Stir through the corn, peas, prawns and reserved marinade from the beef. Continue to stir-fry for a further 1–2 minutes until the rice is well heated. Serve at once.

Note ～ 2 cups of raw rice will produce 6 cups of cooked. You can cook the rice several hours ahead, cover and refrigerate (always be careful to keep cooked rice in the fridge). The rice will then firm up and the grains will remain separate.

Variation ～ Try making a thin two-egg omelette and cutting it into strips. Fold through the mixture when adding the corn, peas and prawns.

Thinly slice the partially frozen beef across the grain, then cut into thin strips.

Add the mushrooms, beef, pork or bacon to the wok and stir-fry over high heat.

~ Porcupine Balls ~

1 cup (220 g/7 oz)
short-grain rice
5 dried Chinese
mushrooms
250 g (8 oz) minced beef
250 g (8 oz) minced
pork
1/3 cup (60 g/2 oz) finely
chopped water
chestnuts
4 spring onions, finely
chopped
1–2 cloves garlic,
crushed

1 teaspoon grated
ginger
1 tablespoon soy sauce
1/2 teaspoon salt
1 egg, lightly beaten

Dipping Sauce
3 tablespoons light
soy sauce
2 tablespoons soft
brown sugar
2 tablespoons grated
fresh ginger

1 ~ Soak the rice in cold water for at least 2 hours, then drain well. Spread to dry on paper towels. Cover the mushrooms with hot water and leave to soak for 20 minutes. Squeeze dry, discard the stems and chop finely.

2 ~ In a large bowl, combine the mushrooms, mince, water chestnuts, spring onions, garlic, ginger, soy, salt and egg. Mix with your hands to combine all the ingredients.

3 ~ Divide the mixture into 20 portions. With wet hands, shape these into small balls. Roll each ball in the rice until well coated. Line a bamboo steamer rack with baking paper and place the balls in the steamer, leaving room for the rice to swell (cook in two or three batches, depending on the size of the steamer). Place the steamer over a wok half-filled with boiling water. Steam for 30 minutes, or until the balls are cooked, adding more water to the wok whenever necessary. Serve Porcupine Balls immediately with Dipping Sauce.

4 ~ **To make Dipping Sauce:** Mix together the soy sauce, brown sugar, fresh ginger and 3 tablespoons water.

Note ~ Steamers and woks are available at Asian shops and are not expensive to buy.

Soak the mushrooms for 20 minutes, then squeeze dry and chop.

Keep your hands wet to avoid sticking when shaping the mixture into balls.

Spread the rice on paper towels or a plate and roll the balls until well coated.

Place the rice balls well apart in the steamer, leaving room for them to swell.

～ Turkish Pilaf ～

Preparation time:
20 minutes + soaking
Total cooking time:
50 minutes

Serves 4–6

2 cups (400 g/12²/₃ oz) long-grain basmati rice	**1 teaspoon ground cumin**
90 g (3 oz) ghee	**1 teaspoon salt**
1 large onion, finely chopped	**1 bay leaf**
1 teaspoon cardamom seeds, lightly crushed	**4 cups (1 litre) hot chicken stock**
1 teaspoon cumin seeds, lightly crushed	**¹/₂ cup (65 g/2¹/₄ oz) shelled pistachio nuts, chopped**
6 whole black peppercorns, lightly crushed	**¹/₂ cup (100 g/3¹/₃ oz) chopped dates**
1 teaspoon turmeric	**¹/₂ cup (100 g/3¹/₃ oz) chopped dried apricots**

1 ～ Wash and soak the rice for 1 hour. Drain in a sieve. Heat the ghee in a large heavy-based pan and add the onion. Cook, stirring, over medium heat for 2–3 minutes until the onion is soft. Add the cardamom, cumin seeds, peppercorns, turmeric, ground cumin, salt and bay leaf. Cook, stirring, for 2–3 minutes to coat the spices with ghee.
2 ～ Stir in the drained rice and cook, stirring continuously, for 2–3 minutes until the rice is well coated with ghee. Gradually pour on the stock, stirring constantly, then bring slowly to the boil. Cook over medium heat for 8–10 minutes, or until almost all the liquid has been absorbed and holes begin to appear on the surface of the rice.
3 ～ Cover with a tight-fitting lid and turn the heat to very low. Cook for 20–25 minutes, or until the rice is cooked. Remove the lid and leave to stand for 5 minutes to allow the steam to escape. Gently fork through the nuts and dried fruit and serve. Delicious with spiced lamb or beef kebabs.
Storage time ～ Best eaten immediately, but will keep for 2 days, covered and refrigerated.
Variation ～ Try almonds, pine nuts or cashews instead of pistachios and use any dried fruit.

Lightly crush the spices and peppercorns with a mortar and pestle or rolling pin.

Soak the rice, then drain well in a sieve and add to the ghee, onion and spices.

Stir the rice with a wooden spoon to coat it well with ghee and spices.

Cook the rice until holes begin to appear on the surface, then cover.

~ Thai-style Steamed Rice ~

Preparation time:
5 minutes
Total cooking time:
25 minutes

Serves 4–6

3 cups (750 ml/24 fl oz) water
2 cups (400 g/12²/₃ oz) fragrant jasmine rice
salt, to taste

1 ~ Slowly bring the water to the boil in a large heavy-based saucepan. Gradually add the rice and salt. Stir and bring back to the boil. Cover with a tight-fitting lid and then reduce the heat to very low and cook for 18–20 minutes. When cooked, remove the lid and allow the steam to escape for 5 minutes. Stir gently with a fork to fluff up the rice. Serve immediately.

Note ~ Rice dries out if left to stand. Leftover rice is best for stir-frying as the dried-out grains separate rather than stick together. Always keep cooked rice in the refrigerator, never at room temperature.

~ Sticky Rice in Coconut Milk ~

Preparation time:
10 minutes + soaking
Total cooking time:
40 minutes

Serves 6–8

2 cups (400 g/12²/₃ oz) white glutinous rice
2¹/₂ cups (600 ml/ 20 fl oz) coconut milk
pinch of salt

1 ~ Put the rice in a large glass or ceramic bowl, cover with water and leave to soak for at least 8 hours or overnight. Wash under running water and then drain well.

2 ~ Line the base and sides of a large bamboo steamer with baking paper or banana leaves. Spread the drained rice evenly over the paper or leaves and cover with the lid. Place the steamer over a wok filled with boiling water up to the base of the steamer. Steam for 20 minutes.

3 ~ Meanwhile, in a large heavy-based pan, heat the coconut milk and salt to just below boiling point. Add the hot rice to the hot coconut milk and stir gently with a fork to combine. Cover with a tight-fitting lid and set aside for 10 minutes, or until the coconut milk has all been absorbed.

4 ~ Spoon the rice back into the steamer. Bring the water to the boil and steam for 10 minutes, or until the rice is cooked. Serve immediately, hot or warm.

Note ~ Good with all Asian foods such as curries. Glutinous rice and bamboo steamers are available from Asian food stores.

Thai-style Steamed Rice (top) and Sticky Rice in Coconut Milk

~ Salmon Coulibiac ~

Preparation time:
25 minutes + chilling
Total cooking time:
1 hour

Serves 4–6

60 g (2 oz) butter
1 onion, finely chopped
200 g (6½ oz) button
  mushrooms, sliced
juice of 1 lemon
200 g (6½ oz) salmon
  fillet, boned and cut
  into small pieces
2 hard-boiled eggs,
  chopped

2 tablespoons fresh dill,
  chopped
3 tablespoons fresh
  parsley, chopped
1 cup (185 g/6 oz)
  cooked brown rice
3 tablespoons cream
375 g (12 oz) packet
  frozen puff pastry
1 egg, beaten

1~Melt half the butter in a frying pan. Add the onion and cook for 5 minutes until soft but not browned. Add the mushrooms and cook for 5 minutes. Add the lemon juice, then remove from the pan.

2~Heat the remaining butter in the pan; add the salmon, stir and cook for 2 minutes. Remove from heat, cool slightly and add the chopped egg, dill, parsley and salt and pepper to taste. Mix gently and set aside. Mix the rice and cream in a small bowl. Set aside.

3~Roll out half the pastry to 15 x 25 cm (6 x 10 inches). Trim the pastry neatly, saving the trimmings, and put on a greased baking tray.

4~Layer the filling onto the pastry, leaving a 3 cm (1¼ inch) border. Put half the rice onto the pastry, then the salmon and egg mixture, followed by the mushroom mixture and finishing with the remaining rice. Brush the border with egg.

5~Roll out the other pastry half to 20 x 30 cm (8 x 12 inches) and place over the filling. Seal the edges. Make two slits in the top of the pie. Decorate with the pastry trimmings and chill for 30 minutes.

6~Preheat the oven to hot 200°C (400°F/Gas 6). Brush the pie with egg and bake for 15 minutes. Reduce the oven to 180°C (350°F/Gas 4); bake for 25–30 minutes, or until golden brown. Serve with sour cream.

Variation~Use a 220 g (7 oz) can of red salmon if more convenient. Freeze for up to one month.

When the salmon has cooled slightly, add the egg, dill, parsley and season to taste.

Roll out the pastry and trim to a neat shape. Reserve the trimmings to decorate.

Spread the remaining rice over the other layers of filling.

Roll out the remaining pastry and place over the filling. Seal with beaten egg.

～ Rice-stuffed Vegetables ～

Preparation time:
40 minutes
Total cooking time:
1 hour 20 minutes

Makes 6

---

2 large tomatoes and
  2 small red or green
  capsicums
1/2 cup (110 g/3²/₃ oz)
  arborio rice
2 tablespoons olive oil
1 red onion, chopped
1–2 cloves garlic,
  crushed
1 teaspoon dried
  oregano leaves
3 tablespoons pine nuts
3 tablespoons currants
1/2 cup (30 g/1 oz)
  chopped fresh basil
3 tablespoons chopped
  fresh parsley
olive oil, to brush

1～Lightly oil a large baking dish. Preheat the oven to warm 160°C (315°F/Gas 2–3). Cut a slice from the top of each tomato. Spoon out the flesh into a bowl, put in a strainer to drain the juice and then finely dice. Reserve the juice and pulp separately. Leave the tomato shells to drain, upside-down, on a rack. Cut the capsicums in half widthways; discard the seeds and membrane. Trim the bases a little so they sit flat—don't cut all the way through.

2～Cook the rice in a large pot of boiling salted water for 10–12 minutes, or until just tender. Drain and set aside in a mixing bowl to cool.

3～Heat the olive oil in a frying pan. Cook the onion, garlic and oregano for 8–10 minutes, or until the onion is tender. Add the pine nuts and currants and cook for a further 5 minutes, stirring frequently. Remove from the heat and stir in the herbs. Season to taste.

4～Add the onion mixture and reserved tomato pulp to the rice and stir well to combine. Fill the tomato and capsicum shells with the rice mixture, piling it up over the top. Spoon 1 tablespoon of the reserved tomato juice on top of the rice and replace the tomato caps.

5～Lightly brush the vegetable shells with olive oil. Arrange the capsicums in a baking dish; cover lightly with foil and bake for 20 minutes. Add the tomatoes and bake for a further 30 minutes, or until cooked. Serve warm or cold.

Spoon the tomato flesh into a bowl, then strain to separate the juice and pulp.

Trim the capsicum bases a little, being careful not to cut all the way through.

Cook the onion, garlic and oregano and then add the pine nuts and currants.

Spoon 1 tablespoon tomato juice over each stuffed vegetable.

～ Cajun Rice ～

Preparation time:
35 minutes
Total cooking time:
45 minutes

Serves 6

60 g (2 oz) butter
1 onion, finely chopped
2 cloves garlic, crushed
1 green capsicum, diced
1 celery stick, diced
180 g (5³/4 oz) chicken livers, chopped
250 g (8 oz) pork mince
3 tablespoons red brown roux (see note)
2 teaspoons chicken stock powder
1 teaspoon Tabasco
1 teaspoon garlic powder
1 teaspoon onion powder
1/2 teaspoon dried thyme leaves
1/2 teaspoon white pepper
1/2 teaspoon cracked black pepper
1/4 teaspoon cayenne pepper
1/4 teaspoon dried oregano
2 cups (400 g/12²/3 oz) long-grain rice
3 cups (750 ml/24 fl oz) chicken stock

1 ～ Heat the butter in a large heavy-based pan. Add the onions, garlic, capsicum and celery. Cook, stirring often, for 5 minutes, or until the vegetables are softened but not browned. Transfer to a plate.

2 ～ Add the livers and pork to the pan. Cook for 2–3 minutes; break up lumps with a fork. Return the vegetables to the pan and cook, stirring, for a further 2–3 minutes. Stir in the red brown roux, stock powder, Tabasco, garlic and onion powders, herbs and spices. Stir well for 1–2 minutes.

3 ～ Stir in the rice and chicken stock. Bring slowly to the boil, then reduce the heat to very low and simmer for 30 minutes, stirring often until the rice is tender. Serve at once.

Note ～ To make red brown roux: Heat 3 tablespoons oil in a heavy-based frying pan. When hot, sprinkle over 3 tablespoons plain flour; mix together then whisk continuously for 3–4 minutes, or until the mixture is nut brown in colour but not burnt. Remove from the pan to stop further cooking. The roux will be very hot so take care. Use a long-handled whisk and an ovenproof cloth to hold the pan steady.

Heat the butter and add the onion, garlic, capsicum and celery.

Add the chicken livers and pork mince, breaking up any lumps with a fork.

Add the red brown roux, stock powder, Tabasco and garlic and onion powders.

To make red brown roux, whisk until the mixture turns nut brown but is not burnt.

~ Sweet Rice Desserts ~

For many of us rice puddings evoke memories of the Sunday roasts of our childhoods—the pudding was traditionally cooked in the bottom of the oven under the meat and vegetables.

Creamy Rice Pudding
Preheat the oven to slow 150°C (300°F/Gas 2). Grease a 1-litre ovenproof dish and put in a baking tin half-filled with water. Wash $1/3$ cup (80 g/$2^2/3$ oz) short-grain rice; drain and combine with 3 cups (750 ml/24 fl oz) full-cream milk, 2 tablespoons caster sugar, 1 teaspoon each vanilla essence and grated lemon rind in the ovenproof dish. Stir well and cover with a lid or foil. Bake for $2^1/2$–3 hours, stirring 3–4 times during cooking. Remove the skin, test that the rice is cooked, then stir in 3 tablespoons cream. Serve warm or cold with stewed fruit. Serves 4–6.

Kheer Rice Pudding
Soak $1/3$ cup (65 g/ $2^1/4$ oz) basmati long-grain rice in water for 30 minutes; drain. Place $1^1/2$ litres full-cream milk and 6 lightly crushed cardamom pods in a large heavy-based pan; bring to the boil. Add the rice, lower the heat and simmer for 1 hour; stir often (the

rice will be soft). Add 125 g/4 oz caster sugar, 1 tablespoon chopped raisins and 3 tablespoons slivered almonds; bring to a low boil and cook for 50 minutes, or until the consistency of porridge. Stir frequently to avoid sticking to the base of the pan. Remove the cardamom pods. Mix a pinch of saffron threads with a little water and add to the mixture—just enough to give a pale yellow colour to the pudding. Stir in 1 tablespoon rose water, if liked, when cooled. Serve warm or cold, with a sprinkling of cinnamon on top. Serves 6.

Danish Rice and Almond Pudding

Place $^1/2$ cup (100 g/ $3^1/3$ oz) long-grain rice and 2 cups (500 ml/ 16 fl oz) cold water in a pan. Stir and bring slowly to the boil. Boil for 2 minutes and then drain. Place $2^1/2$ cups (600 ml/20 fl oz) full-cream milk in a pan and bring slowly to the boil. Add the rice and stir, then reduce the heat to very low simmer. Stir often for 25–30 minutes, or until the rice is cooked. The mixture will be creamy and thick. Remove from the heat; stir in 2 teaspoons

Left to right: Creamy Rice Pudding; Kheer Rice Pudding; Danish Rice and Almond Pudding

vanilla essence and 2 tablespoons caster sugar. Put in a bowl, cover and chill. Beat $^1/2$ cup (125 ml/4 fl oz) cream; fold through the rice with 3 tablespoons chopped slivered almonds. Serve cold topped with a drizzle of cherry liqueur. Serves 4.

～ Sweet Rice Desserts ～

Creamed Rice

Wash $1/2$ cup (110 g/ $3^2/3$ oz) short-grain rice under cold water and drain well. Place 1 litre full-cream milk and $1/3$ cup (90 g/3 oz) caster sugar in a pan. Bring slowly to the boil, stirring until all the sugar has dissolved. Stir in the rice, reduce the heat to very low and cover with a tight-fitting lid. Stir every 15 minutes until the rice is cooked. After about 1 hour the rice will be tender and creamy. Stir in 1 teaspoon vanilla essence. Serve hot or cold with stewed fruit. Serves 4–6.

Old English Rice Pudding

Preheat the oven to warm 160°C (315°F/ Gas 2–3). Lightly grease a 7-cup ovenproof dish with butter. Half fill a baking tin with water and place in the oven. Wash $1/2$ cup (110 g/ $3^2/3$ oz) short-grain rice and leave to drain in a sieve for 10 minutes. Bring $2/3$ cup (170 ml/ $5^1/2$ fl oz) water to the boil in a heavy-based pan; stir in the rice and boil for 2 minutes, or until the water is

absorbed. (Watch the rice does not stick to the pan.) Stir in 1 litre full-cream milk and 1 teaspoon grated lemon rind and then bring to the boil, stirring. Turn down the heat to low and simmer uncovered for 15 minutes, stirring occasionally, or until the rice is cooked. Cool for 5 minutes, then whisk in $2/3$ cup (170 ml/ $5^1/2$ fl oz) thickened cream, 3 egg yolks and 2–3 tablespoons caster sugar to taste.

Left to right: Creamed Rice; Old English Rice Pudding; Baked Rice Custard

Beat 3 egg whites in a small clean bowl until soft peaks form. Gently fold through the rice mixture and then pour into the dish. Place the dish in the baking tin. Bake for 30 minutes, until the mixture is just lightly browned on top. Cover with foil and continue to bake for a further 40–45 minutes, until just firm. Sprinkle with icing sugar and serve warm with extra cream. Serves 4–6.

Baked Rice Custard

Preheat the oven to slow 150°C (300°F/Gas 2). Grease a 1-litre ovenproof dish with melted butter and put in a baking tin half filled with water. Place 1 cup (185 g/6 oz) cooked rice and 3 tablespoons sultanas (optional) in the ovenproof dish. Combine 3 lightly beaten eggs, $2^1/2$ cups (600 ml/20 fl oz) full-cream milk, 1 teaspoon vanilla essence and 3 tablespoons caster sugar and pour over the rice and sultanas.

Bake for 30 minutes, then stir gently with a fork. Cook for a further 30 minutes and stir again. (If you like, sprinkle the surface with ground nutmeg.) Bake for a further 20 minutes, or until the custard is just set. Serve warm or cold. Serves 4.
Note 4 tablespoons of raw rice will yield 1 cup of cooked. Use either short- or long-grain rice.

~ Sticky Black Rice Pudding ~

Preparation time:
10 minutes
+ overnight soaking
Total cooking time:
40 minutes

Serves 6–8

2 cups (400 g/12²/₃ oz)
   black rice
3 fresh pandan leaves
2 cups (500 ml/16 fl oz)
   coconut milk
80 g (2²/₃ oz) palm
   sugar, grated
3 tablespoons caster
   sugar
coconut cream, to
   serve
mango slices or
   pawpaw, to serve

1 Put the rice in a large glass or ceramic bowl and cover with water. Leave to soak for at least 8 hours or overnight. Drain and put in a pan with 4 cups (1 litre) water. Bring slowly to the boil, stirring frequently, and cook at a low boil for 20 minutes, or until tender. Drain.

2 Pull your fingers through the pandan leaves to shred and then tie in a knot. In a large heavy-based pan, heat the coconut milk until almost boiling. Add the palm sugar, caster sugar and pandan leaves and stir until the sugars have dissolved.

3 Add the rice to the pan and cook, stirring, for 3–4 minutes without boiling. Turn off the heat, cover and leave for 15 minutes to absorb the flavours. Remove the pandan leaves. Serve warm with coconut cream and mango or pawpaw slices.

Storage time Best eaten immediately.

Variation Replace the pandan leaves with 1 teaspoon pandan essence if necessary. The long flat leaves of the Pandanus are crushed and used as a flavouring in many Thai sweets. They are sold fresh, frozen, dried or as a flavouring essence or paste. If you can't find pandan, use 1 teaspoon vanilla essence instead. Any fresh tropical fruit, such as banana, pineapple or lychee is also delicious served with this dish.

Note Black rice, palm sugar and pandan leaves are all available from Asian speciality stores.

Palm sugar can be crushed but it is simpler to grate it on a cheese grater.

Leave the black rice to soak overnight, then drain well.

Shred the fresh pandan leaf and then tie in a knot.

Once the rice has absorbed the flavours, lift out the pandan leaves to serve.

～ Empress Rice ～

Preparation time:
45 minutes + chilling
Total cooking time:
1 hour

Serves 6–8

⅔ cup (140 g/4⅔ oz) short-grain rice	4 egg yolks
2 cups (500 ml/16 fl oz) milk	3 tablespoons caster sugar
½ teaspoon vanilla essence	1 teaspoon cornflour
3 tablespoons caster sugar	1 cup (250 ml/8 fl oz) milk
30 g (1 oz) butter	300 ml (9½ fl oz) cream
125 g (4 oz) mixed glacé fruit, chopped	*Apricot Sauce*
2 tablespoons Kirsch	125 g (4 oz) dried apricots
	2 tablespoons Kirsch
Crème Anglaise	1–2 tablespoons caster sugar
1 tablespoon gelatine	

1 ～Lightly grease an 8-cup (2 litre) decorative mould with oil. Put the rice in a pan with 2 cups (500 ml/ 16 fl oz) cold water. Bring slowly to the boil and cook for 2 minutes, then drain. Return the rice to the pan with the milk and vanilla essence. Stir frequently and cook over low heat for 25 minutes, or until the rice is tender and the milk absorbed. Stir in the sugar and butter while hot. Cover and cool. Place the glacé fruit in a bowl, add the Kirsch and soak.

2 ～**To make Crème Anglaise:** Place 2 tablespoons water in a small heatproof bowl, sprinkle with gelatine and leave over hot water until dissolved. Put the egg yolks, caster sugar and cornflour in a large bowl and whisk for 3 minutes until the mixture is pale and thickened. In a pan, heat the milk to scalding point. Pour the milk, whisking continuously, into the egg mixture, then return to the pan. Whisk over low heat until thickened to a thin custard that coats the back of a spoon (take care not to overheat and curdle). Stir in the dissolved gelatine. Cover and cool a little.

3 ～Combine the cooled rice and cooled custard. Beat the cream until firm peaks form. Gently fold the glacé fruit and cream into the rice custard. Spoon into the mould and flatten the surface. Cover and chill for several hours until firm. Unmould onto a plate and serve with Apricot Sauce.

4 ～**To make Apricot Sauce:** Put the apricots in a small pan and cover with water. Leave to soak for 30 minutes, then cook gently for 10 minutes, or until softened. Drain, reserving the liquid. Cool, then purée the apricots in a processor; adding enough cooking liquid to reach sauce consistency. Add Kirsch and sugar to taste.

Storage time ～Cover and refrigerate for up to three days.

Variation ～Try Grand Marnier or Cointreau, instead of Kirsch.

Hint ～To unmould, briefly dip the mould in hot water, wipe dry and then invert onto a serving plate.

Once the rice is tender and the milk absorbed, stir in the sugar and butter.

Heat the milk to scalding point. Pour into the egg mixture, whisking continuously.

～ Thai Sticky Rice ～

Preparation time:
**15 minutes
+ overnight soaking**
Total cooking time:
1 hour

Serves 6–8

2¹/₂ cups (500 g/1 lb)
  glutinous rice
2¹/₂ cups (600 ml/
  20 fl oz) **coconut milk**
¹/₂ cup (125 g/4 oz)
  caster sugar
tropical fruit, to serve

Topping
1 cup (90 g/3 oz)
  desiccated coconut
¹/₄ cup (60 ml/2 fl oz)
  coconut milk, heated
90 g (3 oz) **palm sugar,
  grated**

---

1 ～Put the rice in a large glass bowl and cover with water. Soak for 8 hours or overnight; drain. Line a 30 x 20 cm (12 x 8 inch) shallow tin with non-stick baking paper, overlapping the two long sides. Line a large bamboo steamer with baking paper.

2 ～Spread the steamer base with the rice, put on the lid and place over a wok. Half-fill the wok with boiling water. Steam 45–50 minutes, or until the grains are softened. Top up the wok with water whenever necessary.

3 ～Put the rice, coconut milk and sugar in a large heavy-based pan. Stir over low heat for 10 minutes, or until all the coconut milk is absorbed. Spoon the mixture into the tin and flatten the surface. Set aside to cool and firm.

4 ～**To make Topping:** Put the coconut in a small bowl and mix through the coconut milk. Set aside. Put the palm sugar and 3 tablespoons water in a small pan and stir over low heat until the sugar has dissolved and the syrup thickened a little (3–5 minutes). Stir in the coconut and continue to stir until the mixture holds together. Cover and set aside to cool. Spread the topping over the rice base (or serve separately). Cut into squares or diamonds to serve. Delicious with fresh fruit.

Storage time ～Best eaten on the same day and served at room temperature. Chilling firms the mixture and it loses its flavour.

Note ～Glutinous rice and palm sugar are available from Asian speciality stores. Palm sugar can be grated easily or crushed gently with a rolling pin.

Line the bamboo steamer with greaseproof paper and then spread with rice.

Put the steamer over the wok and half-fill the wok with boiling water.

Spoon the rice mixture into the lined tin and smooth the surface.

Heat the palm sugar and water in a pan then stir in the coconut.

∾ Index ∾